W9-BTR-825

WITHDRAWN

DEMCO

HIPPOS
Huge and Hungry

Lucy Sackett Smith

PowerKiDS
press™
New York

For the Brinkman brothers, who have experience with their own personal hippo.

Published in 2010 by The Rosen Publishing Group, Inc.
29 East 21st Street, New York, NY 10010

First Edition

Editor: Nicole Pristash
Book Design: Kate Laczynski
Photo Researcher: Jessica Gerweck

Photo Credits: Cover, p. 1 Anup Shah/Getty Images; p. 5 © Martin Harvey/Corbis; p. 7 Luca Trovato/Getty Images; p. 9 John Warden/Getty Images; p. 11 Panoramic Images/Getty Images; pp. 12–13 Chris Johns/Getty Images; pp. 15, 21 Shutterstock.com; p. 17 Jonathan and Angela/Getty Images; p. 19 © www.istockphoto.com/ William Bullimore.

Library of Congress Cataloging-in-Publication Data

Smith, Lucy Sackett.
    Hippos : huge and hungry / Lucy Sackett Smith. — 1st ed.
        p. cm. — (Mighty mammals)
Includes index.
    ISBN 978-1-4042-8105-9 (lib. bdg.) — ISBN 978-1-4358-3280-0 (pbk.) —
ISBN 978-1-4358-3281-7 (6-pack)
    1. Hippopotamidae—Juvenile literature. I. Title.
    QL737.U57S65 2010
    599.63'5—dc22
                                    2009002623

Manufactured in the United States of America

CONTENTS

Big and Dangerous

Hippos are some of the world's largest animals. Big, male hippos often weigh as much as 8,000 pounds (3,629 kg)! Hippos have large, round bodies, and they eat mostly grass. These facts make many people think hippos are slow and harmless. However, hippos are quite **aggressive**. They are also very strong. In fact, these huge **mammals** are among the world's most **dangerous** animals.

The word "hippo" is short for "hippopotamus." *Hippopotamus* means "river horse" in Latin. Hippos are not really related to horses, but they do spend much of their time in rivers.

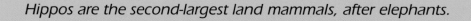

Hippos are the second-largest land mammals, after elephants.

Where Do Hippos Live?

Wild hippos live in Africa. Today, all hippos live south of the Sahara Desert. This sandy desert covers much of northern Africa.

Hippos spend their days resting in the water and their nights eating grass. Therefore, all hippos need to live in a place that has a body of water and nearby grasslands. Many hippos make rivers their daytime homes, while others can be found in lakes or in wetlands. Hippos generally live in freshwater, but a few hippos spend time in the ocean! These hippos can be found off the Arquipélago dos Bijagós, islands that are part of the African country of Guinea-Bissau.

The weather in Africa is very hot. Hippos need to be near water so that they can drink and cool off.

At Home in the Water

Hippos spend as much as 16 hours a day in the water. As all mammals do, hippos breathe air. This means that they have to come up to the water's **surface** to breathe. While under water, adult hippos can easily hold their breath for about 5 minutes. Some hippos can even stay underwater for 30 minutes!

Strangely enough, adult hippos do not generally swim. While young hippos are good swimmers, most grown-up hippos weigh too much to float. Therefore, they do not swim much. Instead of swimming, adult hippos walk or jump along the bottoms of rivers and lakes.

A clear layer called a membrane keeps a hippo's eyes safe and allows the hippo to see underwater.

9

Huge Body, Special Skin

Hippos are huge. They are between 11 and 16 feet (3–5 m) long. A hippo's big body is well suited to its life, though. A hippo's eyes, ears, and **nostrils** are on top of its head. Therefore, a hippo can keep most of its body under water, even when it is breathing or keeping watch for enemies.

Hippos stay underwater as much as they can because their skin dries out easily. A hippo's skin produces a thick, red **liquid**, which is sometimes called blood sweat. This liquid keeps a hippo's skin wet and stops it from getting sunburned when it is outside in the sun.

A hippo's skin dries out easily when it is outside the water.
Pages 12–13: Hippos scare enemies by opening their mouths wide.

MIGHTY FACTS

1 The hippo family is most closely related to a family of animals called cetaceans. Whales and dolphins are cetaceans.

2 Male hippos are called bulls. Females are known as cows.

3 A hippo's nostrils and ears close when the hippo goes underwater.

4 When hippos are sleeping, their bodies come to the surface to breathe and then settle back into the water without the animals having to wake up!

5 Unlike most other animals, hippos talk to each other with sounds that travel both in the water and through the air.

6 People who study hippos now think that the red liquid hippos produce may also keep the animals healthy by killing tiny living things that cause sickness.

7 People are the only animals that commonly hunt adult hippos. However, **hyenas**, lions, and crocodiles eat baby hippos.

8 Hippos are generally about 5 feet (1.5 m) tall.

Life in a Group

Hippos spend their days resting in shallow water in groups of 10 to 30 hippos. Hippo groups may be called herds, schools, bloats, or pods. These groups are made up of mostly females and their young. Most groups also have several young males and one **dominant** older male. Dominant males guard their group against other hippos, and they can be very aggressive.

Hippo groups break up at night when the animals leave the water to find food. Only mothers and their babies stay together to feed. However, the groups form again when morning comes and the hippos return to the water.

This hippo group has gathered in a pool of water in Tanzania, in east Africa. Hippos often do not leave the water at all during the day!

Big Eaters

Even though they spend much of their time in the water, hippos almost always eat on land. Sometimes, hippos will eat fruit, leaves, wood, or dead animals.

Grass is a hippo's main food. Hippos pull up grass with their lips. Then, these big animals smash the grass up with their back teeth.

A hippo can eat more than 85 pounds (39 kg) of food at one time! While that is a lot of food, many other big plant eaters need to eat even more. Hippos do not need to eat as much because they save **energy** by resting in the water.

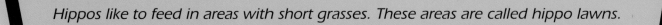
Hippos like to feed in areas with short grasses. These areas are called hippo lawns.

Baby Hippos

Hippos **mate** during the dry season. Therefore, baby hippos are born in the wet season, when there is plenty of food and water. Mother hippos go off by themselves to give birth. Some babies are born on land, but many are born in the water.

Baby hippos are called calves. Newborn calves generally weigh between 50 and 100 pounds (23–45 kg). These big babies nurse, or drink their mothers' milk, both on land and under water.

In the water, tired calves often ride on their mothers' backs. Young hippos generally stay with their mothers until they are about eight years old.

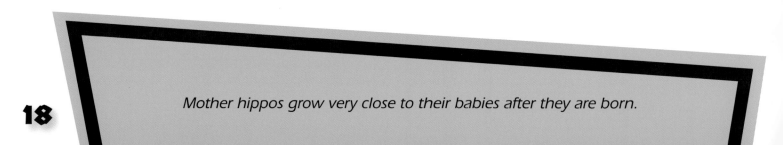

Mother hippos grow very close to their babies after they are born.

Look Out! It's a Hippo!

Mother hippos can be dangerous. They **attack** aggressively when their calves are in danger. Hippos may look slow, but they can run as fast as 30 miles per hour (48 km/h) when charging at an enemy.

The most dangerous hippos are dominant males. They guard their **territories** and fight other males. Hippos fight with their big front teeth, which can grow to be 20 inches (51 cm) long!

To scare off enemies, male hippos open their mouths very wide and show off their teeth. Then, the hippos charge. Most hippo fights take place during the day, while hippos are in the water.

Hippos are very aggressive. It is not uncommon for hippos to hurt each other during fights.

Hippos in Trouble

If they think they are in danger, hippos will attack people. Hippos are believed to attack people more often than any other African animal does. However, people cause problems for hippos, too. People hunt hippos for their teeth, which are used to make decorative objects, and for their meat. Farmers take water for crops from rivers and lakes. This destroys hippos' watery homes.

Hippos are dying out in certain parts of Africa. Hippos have already died out along the Nile River in Egypt, where they lived for thousands of years. Happily, people are now founding parks and **reserves** where these huge animals can live safely!

GLOSSARY

aggressive (uh-GREH-siv) Ready to fight.

attack (uh-TAK) To start a fight with.

dangerous (DAYN-jeh-rus) Might cause hurt.

dominant (DAH-mih-nent) In charge.

energy (EH-nur-jee) The power to work or to act.

hyenas (hy-EE-nuz) Wolflike animals that eat other animals.

liquid (LIH-kwed) Matter that flows.

mammals (MA-mulz) Warm-blooded animals that breathe air and feed milk to their young.

mate (MAYT) To come together to make babies.

nostrils (NOS-trulz) The openings to the nose.

reserves (rih-ZURVZ) Land set aside for wildlife.

surface (SER-fes) The outside of anything.

territories (TER-uh-tor-eez) Land or spaces that animals guard for their use.

INDEX

WEB SITES

Due to the changing nature of Internet links, PowerKids Press has developed an online list of Web sites related to the subject of this book. This site is updated regularly. Please use this link to access the list:
www.powerkidslinks.com/mamm/hippo/